GW00360943

SPIRIT OF
BOURNEMOUTH & POOLE

ROGER HOLMAN

First published in Great Britain in 2010

British Library Cataloguing-in-Publication Data
A CIP record for this title is available from the British Library

ISBN 978 1 906887 32 2

PiXZ Books
Halsgrove House, Ryelands Industrial Estate,
Bagley Road, Wellington, Somerset TA21 9PZ
Tel: 01823 653777
Fax: 01823 216796
email: sales@halsgrove.com

An imprint of Halstar Ltd, part of the Halsgrove group of companies
Information on all Halsgrove titles is available at: www.halsgrove.com

Printed in China by Toppan Leefung Printing Ltd

Introduction

Bournemouth

It all started 180 years ago when Bournemouth was just a small fishing village centred around a cleft in the shoreline through which the little River Bourne ran into the sea.

Captain Lewis Tregonwell who was holidaying at Mudeford with Henrietta his wealthy wife, took her over the dunes to visit this small fishing village. She immediately fell in love with the place so they decided to buy some land and erect themselves a house on the site of what is now The Royal Exeter Hotel.

They enjoyed the location so much with the sandy beach and safe sea bathing that they had built a number of holiday cottages for folks to rent.

The railway arrived in 1870 which gave a huge boost to the number of visitors to the town and economic growth. The mild climate and the softness of the air filtering through the proliferation of pine trees that had been planted, made it an ideal place for recovering from tuberculosis and other aliments. It soon developed a bath chair image which remained until the 1960s when students of Language Schools and the University arrived.

The population grew from 2000 in the 1870s to 60,000 by the turn of the nineteenth century and at the last census stood at 160,000. It is now estimated that over 2 million people visit Bournemouth annually.

Bournemouth Pier

A meeting in 1837 held at the Bath Hotel proposed the building of a pier but due to the lack of finance all they managed to accomplish was a small jetty. Fourteen years later this was replaced by a 1000 feet long wooden construction but alas the marine teredo worm took a liking to it, weakening the structure so much that the pier was washed away over the 1866/67 winter.

Not daunted, a year later the Victorians decided that an iron replacement would reflect the growing importance of the town and also it would be of little interest to the marine wildlife. It was built at a cost of £21,600 and opened by The Lord Mayor of London.

From 1979 to 1981 after surviving two world wars the pier underwent a rebuild in concrete and an addition of an 850 seat pavilion at a cost of £1.7 million.

Just to the east at Boscombe, Europe's first artificial reef is being built. The reef should act as a ramp, pushing the waves upward multiplying their size and improving their quality for surfers, resulting in the doubling of the number of good surfing days.

Bournemouth Pier.

Bournemouth East Cliff.

Bournemouth West Cliff.

This block of flats takes on an impressive appearance at dusk.

Opposite: Beach huts and flats from the pier.

Statue of Lewis Tregonwell erected in front of the Bournemouth International Centre.

Opposite page:
This is where it all started. Captain Lewis Tregonwell built his house here on the site of what is now The Royal Exeter Hotel.

Above left: The upper gardens. *Above right:* The view from the upper gardens of the memorial and St Stephen's Church. The church was designed by J.L.Pearson and according to Betjeman "worth travelling 200 miles and being sick in the coach to see the inside of the church". The outside looks impressive too.

Opposite: Bournemouth lower gardens look attractive at all times but particularly in spring and summer when the flowers are in full bloom.

The Bournemouth Eye is a tethered helium-filled balloon, ascending from the lower gardens and lifting passengers to a height of 500 feet providing panoramic views over the whole area to a distance of 40 km.

The glorious sweep of the Bournemouth bay to Poole Harbour entrance with the ferry just visible.

Looking towards the New Forest.

Opposite: Bournemouth to Hengistbury Head.

An early spring day before the visitors arrive. The distant Purbeck Hills provide
a beautiful backdrop, creating an intimate atmosphere for the seafront.

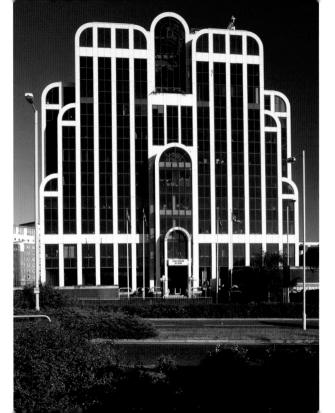

The McCarthy & Stone
building seems reminiscent
of a pre-war radio.

Branksome Chine.

Lower Gardens with the Pavilion in the background. Before the Bournemouth International Centre was built the Pavilion was the main location for entertainment in Bournemouth hosting dances and shows. I wonder how many romances started there.

Holdenhurst village became a cul-de-sac when the Bournemouth spur road was built. It has an attractive little church and is the only place I know to still use gas street lamps.

Opposite: Sandbanks to Bournemouth with a heavy sea running.

The entrance to the new seafront development at Boscombe.

Opposite: Bournemouth Pier.

Boscombe Pier.

The Isle of Wight can just be seen through the arches.

The new flat development along the seafront.

Opposite: Sunrise Bournemouth looking toward Boscombe Pier and Hengistbury Head.

Poole

Poole has a population of 138,000 and is situated beside the second largest natural harbour in the world. Both Poole and Bournemouth have expanded to meet each other, making it one big conurbation.

The harbour, although large at approximately 100 miles in circumference, is very shallow exposing acres of sand banks at low tide, making it ideal for wildlife but not for large ships who need to ply in and out of the harbour. Consequently there is a need for almost continuous dredging to keep the channels open

The Poole Harbour area has been inhabited for over 2000 years. The local tribe were the Celtic Durotriges who lived in Dorset in the Iron Age, particularly around Wareham, which was initially a much more important port but with the river channel silting up and larger boats being built, it gradually subsided as Poole became the major port.

In the early seventeenth century Poole became very prosperous due to its connection with the Newfoundland trade, and it continued thus well into the next century. It then declined although there was some revival coinciding with the economic growth of Bournemouth, but it had to wait until the 1960s for it to regain its real prosperity with the introduction of container traffic and the location to the town of a number of successful companies including Barclays International, Hamworthy Engineering, Sunseeker to name a few.

The harbour being so vast, shallow and weather protected has become a favourite with sailors and wind surfers.

Brownsea is largest of the islands in Poole Harbour and is now owned by The National Trust. It has had a colourful history since Henry VIII built a blockhouse there as part of his coastal defence system. In the seventeenth century, copperas was produced on the island and during the eighteenth the blockhouse was transformed into an imitation castle. In1852 Colonel Waugh became the owner and set up a manufacturing capacity producing drainage and sewerage pipes. Alas he went bankrupt and it was then bought by a succession of owners. In 1897 the castle was burnt down and rebuilt in 1901. From 1927 until 1961 it was owned by the very reclusive Mrs Bonham-Christie who allowed Brownsea to become a wilderness with strict instructions to her staff to allow no one to land on the island. There are sika deer and a red squirrel population with the whole of the north of the island managed by the Dorset Wildlife Trust and the RSPB.

Brownsea landing stage and National Trust properties.

Brownsea Castle. Now leased to The John Lewis Partnership as a high class holiday hotel for their staff, it has a two-year waiting list.

Sandbanks Ferry.

The Haven, harbour entrance and chain ferry.

Harbour sunset.

Kite surfing in the harbour has become very popular in recent years because of its ideal location.

A new development on the site of the old Poole Pottery which has not gained universal approval.

Above left: Barclays International built these office blocks when they located to Poole in 1957.
Above right: This is the statue of Lord Baden-Powell sitting on the quay looking over to Brownsea Island where he set up the very first Scout camp and then proceeded to introduce Scouting around the world.

There is a small harbour within a harbour which is reserved for the boats of working fishermen.

Opposite: Looking toward Evening Hill with the tide out.

The Custom House on the Quay.

Opposite:
In early 2009 the water near the shore at Sandbanks froze and when thawing, created these small ice floes. A very unusual occurrence.

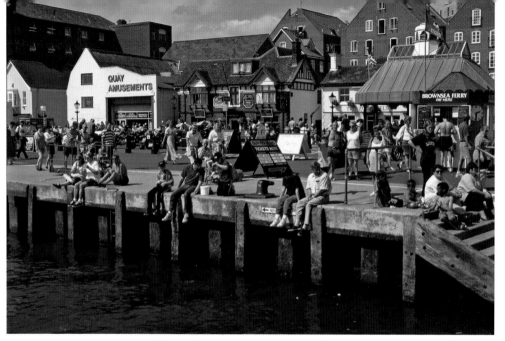

In summer, locals and visitors alike congregate to watch all the activity on the quayside.

Early morning picture taken from the lifting bridge.

The Mansion House,
one of the town's magnificent
Georgian houses, probably
built for a prosperous
Poole trader.

Fortunately The Guildhall survived the rush to demolish much of the old town after World War II. It is now a museum and is an impressive building built in 1761 with its grand curving stairways.

Statue standing outside the new ASDA shopping and flat development.

Sunseeker yachts standing in front of one of their manufacturing yards. Sunseeker is one of the biggest employers in Poole, manufacturing and selling luxury boats all around the world.

The *Tenacious* in harbour.

Poole Quay land train.

Brownsea from Evening Hill.

The harbour at low tide with calm water and a magnificent sunset.

The popularity of board surfing has probably declined with the increase of kite surfing.

Shore Road, Sandbanks, claimed to be the most valuable property in the country if not the world. It is ironic to reflect that 100 years ago the whole lot could probably have been purchased for what is now no more than an average weekly wage.

House boats just inside the harbour entrance.

Opposite: Sandbanks early morning.

Wytch Farm Oilfield. The biggest on-shore oilfield in Western Europe.

Cobbs Quay seen from across Holes Bay.

Upton House and Country Park is situated on the northwest edge of Poole Harbour and is owned by Poole Council. It has had a chequered history with its main claim to fame being that it was the subject of the longest-running dispute in legal history.

Poole Harbour Yacht Club.

Looking toward Old Harry and the Purbecks from Sandbanks.